BETTER FISHING
for Boys

JAMES P. KENEALY

DODD, MEAD & COMPANY • NEW YORK

To my Friend Rudy Richter who also believes our young people must learn to use, care for, and love our great outdoors

Jim Kenealy

CONTENTS

This book is dedicated to Jack Curtis and the memory of Jack Barrett who, many years ago, found the time to take a small boy fishing.

While writing this book, many people and companies gave generously of their time and products. The following have been especially helpful: James McDonald for his assistance and guidance with the photography; my fishing mates, Rodger Buonanno and John Salonis, fishermen par excellence; Berkley and Company; Cortland Line Company; The Garcia Corperation; Penn Fishing Tackle Company; Plano Molding Company; Scientific Anglers Inc.; Wright and McGill Company; and Zebco Inc. Also to Angie, Nancy, Mike, and Deane who share my love of the outdoors.

SPORT FISHING

Fishing is the most popular recreational pastime in the world. In the United States alone, almost 70 million people are fishing enthusiasts. Of this number, nearly one half are boys. Even more significant is the fact that 80% of all fish caught are taken by 20% of the fishermen. This proves fishing is not luck, but a combination of "know how" and skill.

To make sure you become one of the 20%, decide first on a method of fishing, either spin or bait casting, spinning or fly fishing. Then learn to use your equipment efficiently, explore local waters and study the habits of the fish in them.

Of the four ways to fish, spin casting is the easiest to learn with spinning a close second. Bait casting and fly casting require more skill, but with a little practice and patience can also be quickly mastered.

To help make the right choice, ask the advice of local fishermen, outdoor editors, and established fishing tackle dealers. They know your local waters and how best to fish them. They can also recommend a balanced outfit (rod, reel, line, baits, lures), suited to your area.

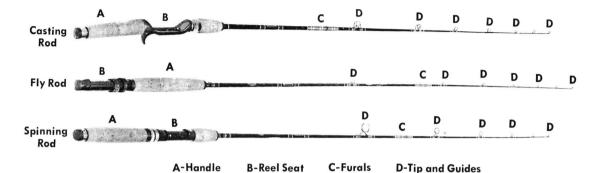

A-Handle   B-Reel Seat   C-Furals   D-Tip and Guides

When purchasing a rod, carefully inspect points A through D.

HOW TO SELECT YOUR EQUIPMENT

Buying fishing equipment, especially your first outfit, is always an exciting time. It can, however, become a problem unless you know how to select the right equipment. Things to look for are quality materials, good workmanship, and balanced tackle. The surest way to get a "right" outfit is to buy recognized name brand equipment at an established fishing or sporting goods store.

The cost of a good starter outfit (rod, reel, line) can be kept below $20 with an additional $2 to $5 for hooks, leaders, lures, etc.

Materials and Construction

Rods—Most fishing rods made today are constructed of hollow or solid fiberglass shafts, cork or wood and metal handles, tempered metal furals and line guides. Tonkin cane shafts, a bamboo wood, is used by a few companies specializing in custom rods.

When inspecting a rod, check for the following:

A. Handle should be comfortable to grip and the cork or wood well glued to prevent twisting or slipping.

B. Reel seats should have a strong, positive locking device to prevent any reel movement when playing a fish.

C. Furals should slip in and out snugly with a firm steady push or pulling pressure. Never use a twisting motion when taking them apart unless the manufacturer recommends it. The ends that are permanently affixed to the rod sections must fit tight and be well-glued to prevent twisting or slipping.

D. Line guides and tips should be firmly attached to the rod with glue and winding thread. The tip and guides should lie in a straight line along the rod to

ROD ACTIONS

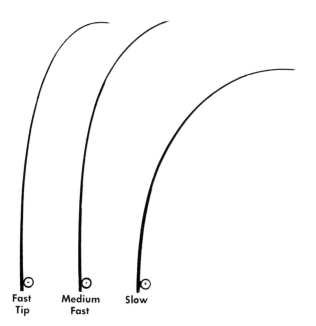

Fast Tip   Medium Fast   Slow

Medium fast action rods are recommended for new fishermen.

ensure a straight, even flow of line when casting.

After inspecting the rod, slowly flex it. Look for sharp bends along the curve. These are weak spots in the rod and will make accurate casting impossible. While still holding the rod, bring it up to eye level and slowly revolve it in your hands. The shaft should be straight and even with just a slight downward bend at the tip. Heavy duty and short rods will not have this bend.

Action—Every fishing rod has a certain action or flex built into the shaft, the purpose being to assure better casting accuracy and/or distance. The three most common actions are "Fast tip," "Slow," and "Medium Fast." In a "fast tip" action rod the top section does most of the flexing and snaps back quickly on the cast. This encourages greater distance, but some accuracy is sacrificed because lure or line "feel" is lost in the stiff butt section.

In slow or soft action rods the flex tends to be uniform from tip to butt, giving a smooth slow action. This allows maximum lure/line "feel," making pinpoint accuracy possible but some loss of distance. Medium fast action rods, depending on the manufacturer, fall somewhere between "fast Tip" and "Slow," allowing accuracy plus distance. These are the general purpose rods designed for average fishermen who do not have the time or money to develop a fishing arsenal. The one drawback to the medium action rods is that each manufacturer develops his own action which can be confusing to a new fisherman. Here again is where advice from an experienced fisherman friend or reputable dealer will save you a lot of headaches. They will also interpret the special names most manufacturers give their various rod actions.

Reels—Fishing reels take more use and abuse than any other piece of fishing equipment. They must store line, release line with a minimum of effort, act as a break on fighting fish and lastly, reel in the fish as he tires. The fact they do these things well is a tribute to the designers and manufacturers.

When inspecting a reel check for the following:

All metal and plastics used in the construction should be rust and/or corrosion resistant. All grease and oil nipples should be easily reached from the outside of the reel.

A. The reel foot should fit and lock tightly in the reel seat of the rod.

B. Handles should be large enough to grip easily and turn with a minimum of effort.

C. Level wind arms and bail pickups should distribute the line evenly on the spool and be made of extra hard tempered metal.

D. Spools should have a minimum clearance at the reel housing and be wide or deep enough to hold ample line. If the spool feels "sloppy," chances are line will slip down behind the spool walls.

E. Adjustable drag (brake) should be easy to reach and adjust without disassembling any part of the reel.

F. All better reels have a "click" warning device that alerts you when the reel is turning. This is usually a small button or lever that slides on or off.

Most good reels will have a "quick take down" feature which lets you disassemble the reel quickly and with a minimum of effort. This feature is especially helpful if dirt or sand gets into the reel housing and must be cleaned while fishing.

Lines—The type and weight (breaking strength) line you use will depend on your method of fishing, and the size fish you expect to catch. Bait casting calls for either hard braided nylon line or, on special spools, a monofilament line. Spin casting and spinning use the new soft monofilament lines. Trolling lines are made from nylon, dacron, linen, monofilament, monel wire, or lead core.

Fly lines are made with nylon or silk cores and are coated with special plastic finishes that make them float or sink depending on the purpose. In fly fishing, the weight and taper of the line rather than the lure

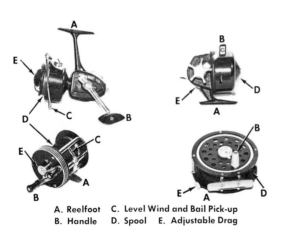

A. Reelfoot   C. Level Wind and Bail Pick-up
B. Handle   D. Spool   E. Adjustable Drag

When purchasing a reel, make a careful inspection at points A through E.

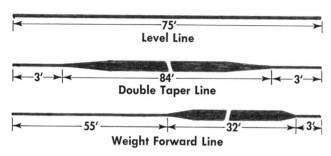

FLY LINES

Level Line — 75'

Double Taper Line — 3' | 84' | 3'

Weight Forward Line — 55' | 32' | 3'

The "Weight Forward" line is recommended for learning and general fly fishing.

makes casting possible. This means many different size and tapered lines are necessary to match the various length and actions of today's fly rods.

The three most common fly lines are: the level line which has no taper, the double tapered line which is heaviest in the middle tapering down to equal smaller diameters at each end, and the weight forward taper line which has the heaviest part of the line up front. Of the three, the weight forward line is recommended for use while learning to fly cast. The level line is the most inexpensive but should never be used while learning. Even accomplished fly casters find it difficult to "throw." The double taper is an excellent line but takes a bit more skill to "throw" than a weight forward line. When selecting a fly outfit, make sure the line matches the rod. All better rod manufacturers designate the size line to

use with their various rods. This information is usually marked on the rod just above the handle or in an attached information card.

As most fly lines are only twenty-five to thirty-five yards long a backing line between the spool and fly line is recommended to protect against a long run by a fish. One or two hundred yards of nylon line (10 to 20 pound test) makes a good backing line.

Leaders—A leader is the piece of monofilament or wire placed between the hook or lure and the line. The main purpose of monofilament is to act as an invisible connection and fool fish, into thinking the bait or lure is swimming free. Wire leaders, on the other hand, are used when fishing for large and/or sharp toothed fish that might cut or break the line.

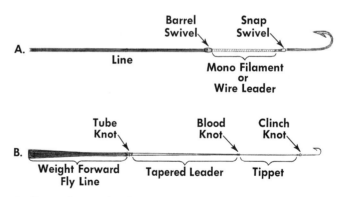

A. Shows how a leader is rigged between the line and hook. B. Shows how to rig a tapered leader and tippet to a fly line.

11

In fly fishing, tapered leaders and tippets are used as an invisible extension of the casting line. The butt end (end tied to the line) should be at least ⅔ the diameter of the end of the line and taper down to ½ or less the diameter.

The tippet, a short piece of monofilament, is used to keep from shortening the leader as it is necessary to cut the tippet each time you change flies.

Tapered leaders come in 6-7½-9-12-15 foot lengths. Tippets are usually made 1½ to 2 feet long.

Hooks—The size, type and design hooks you use will depend on the type fishing being done. Small hooks are used on small fish. Extra strong small hooks, medium and large hooks, are used to catch large fish. Two popular type hooks for general use are the Sproat and the Eagle Claw designs in sizes 7/0 through 10. Figure 7 and 7A shows other widely used designs and a hook size chart.

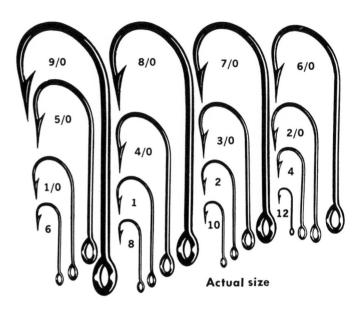

Actual size

Hook chart.

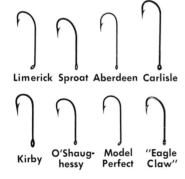

Limerick Sproat Aberdeen Carlisle

Kirby O'Shaug-hessy Model Perfect "Eagle Claw"

Various type hooks. The Sproat and Eagle Claw design are excellent general purpose hooks.

A. Improved Clinch Knot
Used to tie monofilament leaders or tippets to hooks, lures, and other metal eyes. This is a favorite knot with fly fishermen.

B. Eye Knot
Used to tie line or leaders to hook or other metal eye. To insure against slipping tie a keeper knot (overhand) at the end of the line.

C. Blood Knot
Used to tie two leaders or lines of about the same diameter. Note: The lines are twisted in opposite directions. When twisted in the same direction, the result is a barrel knot, inferior to the blood knot.

A

B

C

D. Tube or Nail Knot

Used to join a leader and fly line. This knot is far superior to a jamb knot.

To Tie: Lay thin tube or nail beside the fly line. Make ten or twelve turns around fly line and tube with heavy end of leader. Slip the short end of leader back through the tube or alongside the nail. Then slide the tube out of the knot and pull the leader up tight with a slow even pressure.

E. Key's Knot

Use to join monofilament leaders to braided line.

F. Surgeon's Knot

Use to tie two different or similar lines together.

FISHING KNOTS

Knowing how and when to use the right knot is often the difference between landing or losing a fish, especially when tying monofilament and other synthetic lines. Each of these man-made fibers have certain characteristics that make special knots necessary to insure holding. A few of the better fishing knots and where to use them are shown in Figure 7B.

Recommended baits and lures are covered on pages 48-53 ("Favorite Lures and Baits").

HOW TO SELECT YOUR FISHING ACCESSORIES

Fishing accessories are the "extras" that make sport fishing more enjoyable and comfortable. So once your basic tackle is bought, start listing in the order of importance, the accessories you will want. Develop a check list showing general equipment and specialized items. Then as you save or earn money to buy an accessory, your list will show what you need. A check list also makes an ideal present reminder for birthdays and other special occasions.

Following is a master check list. Use it as a guide to develop your accessories list. General: Fishing tackle box, jackknife, rod case, hook degouger, reel pouch, fishing pliers, tackle repair kit, insect repellent, landing net, hook sharpening stone, boots or waders, comfortable wool socks for boots, hat for sun and rain (one that will not blow off in a wind), lightweight comfortable rainwear, cooler (to transport fish), chain or line fish keeper, polaroid sun glasses.

Plano #8600 fishing box loaded with lures and accessories.

13

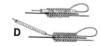

A. Shows a well-designed reel seat with double locking rings.

Bait or Spin Casting—extra hooks, line and leaders, bobbers (various sizes), lead weights (various weights and sizes), bait box, bait pail, minnow trap, gaff.

Spin Fishing—Extra hooks and leaders, extra spools and lines, pocket lure box, belt bait box, bobbers (various sizes), lead weights (various sizes and weights).

Fly Fishing—Extra hooks, tippets and leaders (6'-9' sizes 4-8 lb. test), assorted split shot weights, fishing vest, canvas creel, extra line (sinking weight forward taper), fly line dressing, line drier, leader cutter (fingernail clipper), pocket fly box, leader container, Orvis knot tying pocket vise, Eagle Claw Tie focal.

HOW TO BALANCE EQUIPMENT

To get top performance from your equipment, the rod, reel, line, and lures should all work as a unit. Experienced fishermen call this balancing or matching tackle and consider it the key to developing accuracy and distance when casting.

Fortunately, today's fishing tackle can be balanced easily. Most rods state what action they have, and recommend line size or lure weight. This in turn helps decide what size reel is needed.

The important things to check when balancing an outfit are:

A. The rod and reel should have a comfortable feel (balance and weight) when you go through the casting motion. They should also be sized to meet the fishing demands that will be put on them. Example! An ultralight rod would use a small reel with light line, whereas large salt water rods need rugged large capacity reels and heavy line.

B. The reel should lock firmly onto the rod's reel seat. Any play or looseness means the reel foot is too small or the locking device is poorly designed.

C. Line should fill the reel spool to within about 1/16th inch of the top. This encourages greater casting distance because fewer spool revolutions are necessary to reach a mark. It also stores extra line, often needed when playing a fighting fish. The line should also leave the spool smoothly, moving up through the rod guides with a minimum of friction. When more than one spool of line is used to fill a reel make sure the line is continuous. Never tie lines together except in an emergency.

Note: Line/spool ratio is not necessary in fly fishing as the reel is not used when casting.

D. Lures and fly lines should fall into the weight range recommended by the rod manufacturer. Failure to do this causes a rod to act stiff or sluggish when casting.

Following are some recommended matched outfits developed for general all around fishing. Use them as a guide when selecting your own tackle.

Spin Casting

Rods—5½ to 6 foot long, medium fast action, designed to handle lures ¼ to ⅝ oz. Spin and Bait casting rods are interchangeable, but the guides on spin casting rods are a bit larger. Look and ask for this feature. Line: 6 to 10 lb. test soft monofilament, minimum 100 yards.

Reel—Large enough to hold the recommended length and size line. Rugged enough for the type fishing planned. Comfortable to your grip. Easy to thumb the push button line release. Crank and handles easy to reach and turn.

Leaders—1 to 3 feet long, soft monofilament or wire line. When using monofilament leaders, have the breaking strength slightly less than the line. This allows the leader to break rather than the line, should you get hung up. Wire leaders are used on sharp-toothed fish (pike, muskie, etc.).

Lures—¼ to ⅝ oz. plugs, spoons and spinners. (See "Favorite Lures and Baits," Page 49.)

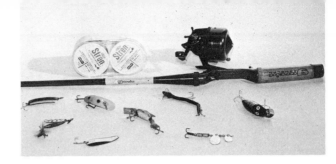

Matched Spin Casting Outfit. Garcia #2624 B-6′ spin cast rod, #170 Garcia "Abu-Matic" reel, 200 yards of 8 lb. test monofilament line, assorted lures (¼ to ⅝ oz.)

Spinning

Rod—6½ to 7 foot long, medium fast action, designed to handle lures ¼ to ⅝ oz.

Reel—Large enough to hold the recommended size and length of line. Rugged enough for the type fishing planned. Foot and leg comfortable to hold; line easy to pick up when ready to cast; crank and handle easy to reach and turn.

Line—6 to 10 lb. test monofilament, minimum 100 yards.

Leaders—2 to 4 feet long, soft monofilament or wire line. (See spin casting leaders.)

Lures—Assorted ¼ to ⅝ oz. plugs, spoons and spinners. (See "Favorite Lures and Baits," Page 49.)

Bait Casting

Rod—5 to 5½ feet long, medium fast action, designed to handle lures ⅜ to ¾ oz.

Matched Spinning Outfits. (Regular and Ultra-light) Top: Berkley "420" reel, Berkley P30ML 7' "Para/Metric" spinning rod, 200 yards of 8 lb. test monofilament line, assorted lures (¼ to ⅝ oz.) Bottom: Garcia Ultra-light spinning outfit; #408 Mitchell reel, #2500 B 5' Ultra-light spinning rod, 200 yards 4 lb. test line, assorted lures (⅛ to ¼ oz.)

Reel—Large enough to hold recommended size and length of line; rugged enough for the type fishing planned; reel set low on reel seat to allow easy thumbing of spool; handles easy to reach and turn; spool when spinning should rotate with a minimum of drag; level wind guide should lay line evenly on spool when retrieving (winding line back on spool).

Line—10 to 15 lb. test hard braided nylon, minimum 100 yards.

Leaders—1½ to 4 feet long, soft monofilament or wire line (see spin casting leaders).

Lures—Assorted ⅜ to ¾ oz. plugs, spoons and spinners. (See "Favorite Lures and Baits," Page 49.)

Fly Casting

Rod—7½ to 8 feet long, medium action.

Line—WF6F or line size specified by rod manufacturer. (See fly lines, Page 11.)

Reel—Large enough to hold the recommended size line plus 150 or more feet of backing line (15 lb. braided nylon or dacron). When using a single action reel, the handle should be comfortable to grip and turn. With an automatic action reel, be sure the spring winding wheel tightens the spring mechanism quickly and smoothly, and the trigger release arm is easy to reach and work.

Leaders and Tippets—1X, 2X and 3X tapered leaders 6 and 7½ feet long, 2X, 3X, 4X, 5X and 6X tippet material (8 or 10 yard coils).

Lures—Assortment of dry and wet flies, streamers, poppers, nymphs, etc. (See "Favorite Lures and Baits," Page 53.)

Salt Water Tackle

If you live by the ocean, chances are much of your fishing will be done in salt water. The tackle you use will be similar to fresh water equipment, the only difference being size and degree of corrosion resist-

Matched Bait Casting Outfit. Zebco Steamlight reel, Zebco #3366 5½' bait casting rod, 150 yards of 12 lb. test nylon braided line, assorted lures (⅜ to ¾ oz.)

Matched Fly Casting Outfits (Regular and light) Top: Berkley P40 8' Para/Metric fly rod #510 Berkley reel, #8 Cortland Weight forward floating line, assorted tapered leaders and flies. Bottom: Fenwick #FF60 6' Fly rod #1492 Pfluger Medalist reel, #5 weight forward Scientific Anglers floating line, assorted tapered leaders and flies.

ance. Salt water tackle is usually larger because ocean fish are bigger and all metal parts must have extra protection against salt corrosion. You can, however, use your fresh water tackle for occasional salt water use if it has anodized or corrosion resistant metal parts. Just be careful not to go after fish too large for your outfit and be sure to rinse it well in fresh water after each use. Salt water tackle should also be rinsed.

Trolling Tackle

In trolling, you pull or tow your lure behind a slow moving boat. This eliminates the need to cast and allows you to cover a much larger water area. Except for certain species of fish (salt water big game, etc.) any basic outfit can be used for trolling. Just be careful, as in salt water fishing, not to go after fish too large for your outfit. If you live in an area where trolling is the popular method of fishing,

Salt Water Matched Outfits: A. Big game offshore trolling rig, used to catch large fish in the 500 lb. class. Penn Senator #9 reel, Montague 6½' "Big Game" rod 400 yards of 80 lb. test. B. Salt water bait casting rig used for surf casting, trolling or still fishing. Penn "Leveline" reel, true temper Super Magnum 7' rod; 250 yards of 30 lb. test. Berkley Dacron "Medallion" line. C. Fresh water bait casting rig shows the greater size of salt water equipment.

you may want to get a trolling rig. The rod should be 4½ to 6½ feet long and have a stiff action; the reel should have a large line capacity with a heavy drag clutch. Lines must be a good quality monofilament, trolling wire, hard braided nylon or dacron. The size and breaking strength will be determined by the type of fish you are going after.

Trolling Outfit: Wright-McGill 5' "Muskie" rod, Penn "leveline" reel, 250 yards of 30 lb. test Berkley Dacron "Medallion" line, assorted lures.

HOW TO CARE FOR AND MAINTAIN YOUR EQUIPMENT

Surveys show more fish are lost because of tackle failure than any other reason. This is especially true of trophy catches, as large fish put the greatest strain on equipment. To avoid this pitfall, take a cue from the experts and use their ten-minute care and preventive maintenance program. All you must do is inspect, clean, and, if necessary, oil or grease your tackle after each outing. In most instances you won't spend ten minutes, which is in itself a tribute to today's quality-built and trouble-free fishing equipment.

Begin the inspection on your last cast of the day. Make it a long one, so that lots of line runs out. Then as you start to retrieve, let the line slide between your thumb and forefinger. This will clean off any slime or heavy dirt and is an excellent way to feel for breaks, pinches, kinks, or wind knots. These are all weak spots and should be removed or the line cut back to that point. Pay special attention to the knots that join the line and leader together and where the hook ties to the leader. Actually, if you are fishing for sharp-toothed fish or around stumps and weeds, it's a good idea to check the leader periodically and replace the lower section of any monofilament leader after each hard fishing session.

Once the line is retrieved and the hook or lure removed from the leader, take the reel off the rod and disassemble your rod for cleaning. Wipe down and dry each section, then inspect for the following: loose ferrules or guides, wrappings that are cut or unwinding, worn or sharp spots on guides or tip, and cracks, dents or splits on the shaft. Also check the handle for loose screws or plugs and make sure the reel seat locking device works smoothly. If everything checks out okay, place the rod in its cloth bag and metal or fiber case until your next outing. Never store rods or any other tackle in moisture-proof plastic bags. Over long storage periods condensation can cause some rusting on metal parts.

Next, inspect your reel for loose or worn parts, rinse in clean water, shake, and wipe dry, then put a drop or two of oil in each oiling nipple. Be careful not to get any oil on the line. Always store the reel in a cloth or leather bag, never in a moisture-proof plastic bag. While fishing, if any sand or grit gets into the reel's mechanism, stop fishing and clean it

To clean the line and check for kinks, knots, or breaks, make a habit of occasionally sliding the line through your thumb and forefinger while retrieving. Always do so on the last cast of the day.

thoroughly. Most reels have a quick take down assembly which makes cleaning simple. Under no circumstances, try to use the reel until it is cleaned and turning smoothly.

In areas where the water is extremely dirty or salty, wait until you get home or back to camp before cleaning your equipment. Then wash each piece in mild soapy water, rinse well in clean water, dry thoroughly, and where necessary, oil or grease.

When major repairs are needed, bring the equipment to a tackle repair shop. On minor problems, fix them yourself with the help of an experienced fisherman.

Winter Overhaul

At least once a year give your equipment a complete overhaul. Wash down the rod and clean the reel with a good nontoxic, noninflammable cleaning solution. Then grease and oil the reel with a good reel lubricant. Remove the line from the reel spool, wash it in a mild soap solution, then rinse in clean water and dry. Never use a petroleum base cleaner on synthetic fly lines. If the line passes inspection, reel it back on the spool starting with the front end. This is called line reversing and can be done on all lines except a weight forward fly line.

After your basic tackle is cared for, start on the accessories. Clean, paint, repair, sharpen, polish, and patch wherever necessary and throw away all the "junk" that finds its way into every tackle box each season.

Care and Maintenance Tips

Following are some tips that will help protect and keep your equipment in A-1 condition:

1. Keep your hooks sharpened by occasionally touching them up with a hook sharpening stone.

2. Never lay a rod on the ground where it might get stepped on or the reel and line might become dirty.

3. Use paraffin wax to lubricate ferrules, never use oil, and when a ferrule becomes stuck, free it with a nontoxic, noninflammable fluid. Separate ferrules with a straight, slow, steady, pulling motion, never a twisting motion unless recommended by the manufacturer.

4. Be careful of the tip when carrying an assembled rod. They have a habit of getting caught in closing doors, jammed into the ground or snagged in high grass or bushes.

5. Keep your tackle box latched when not in use. This keeps the contents in place should it be accidentally tipped over or picked up quickly.

6. Some bug repellents, fly dope, suntan lotions, etc., will soften synthetic lines, varnish and paint, so do not store any of these items in your tackle box. Carry them in a pocket.

7. Always carry and learn to use an emergency repair kit. It should contain: tip cement, guide wrapping tape, grease and oil, tools (knife, pliers, screwdriver, and reel wrench), and a small coil of soft wire.

HOW TO CAST

Casting is the art of accurately throwing or propelling a lure to a distant spot. How well you learn this art will decide, to a great degree, your skill as a fisherman. Experience has shown that the angler with fishing know-how and a good casting arm will always out-fish the poor to average caster. He also has more fun. So plan now to practice until you can drop a lure on the proverbial dime at twenty paces.

In fishing, there are four basic methods of casting: spin casting, spinning, bait casting, and fly casting. Although each has certain procedures that differ

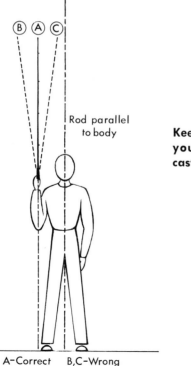

Rod parallel to body

Keep rod parallel to your body while casting.

A-Correct B,C-Wrong

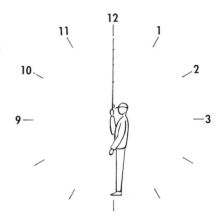

The clock face method is the best and quickest way to learn how to cast.

from those of the others, many techniques are common to all four methods and should be understood before you start practicing. Distance is achieved by the amount of bend and snapback you get from your rod, while accuracy is developed by coordinating arm and rod movement in a plane parallel to your body. Or to put it another way, when moving the rod backward and forward the tip should not wander to the right or left. This parallel rod movement shoots the lure out over the water in a straight line on target.

The quickest and easiest way to learn casting is by using the clock face system. Picture yourself standing in front of a large clock, your feet at 6:00 and the rod acting as the hour hand. When held vertical, the rod will read 12:00. When held horizontal, it will read 9:00 and be pointing to your target. With this system, rod movements are easily emphasized by the hour numerals and your body is always facing the target.

Drag Set

Every well-made reel (small fly reels excepted) has a built-in line braking system called a drag clutch. This mechanism, usually a friction plate controlled by a knob or starwheel, makes it possible to increase or decrease the amount of pressure a fighting fish must exert to pull line from the reel. Although setting or adjusting the drag has no bearing on casting, it is a good idea at this time to learn where the drag is located and how it works on your reel. This information will be included in the directions that come with the reel. The tension at which to set the drag is covered under: "How to Fight and Land a Fish" on page 46.

Spin Casting

Spin casting is the easiest method of fishing to learn because the reel is practically foolproof. Actually, anyone with a little coordination can make amazingly accurate casts after just a few minutes of practice. This is why most experts recommend spin casting to new fishermen and the occasional angler.

Once your tackle is assembled, including a practice plug, reel in the line until the plug hangs just a few inches from the rod tip. Then grasp the rod handle so your thumb can comfortably reach the push button on the reel. Next, point the rod in a horizontal

9:00 position and turn your wrist until the reel handle faces up (down for left-handers). This is the starting position for all overhead spin casts.

Before starting to cast, take a minute or two and get acquainted with the reel. With the rod at 9:00, push the line release button to open the line pickup pin. Next, release the button, and the practice plug will fall to the ground. To stop the plug before it hits the ground, push the reel button which acts as a line brake. To retrieve the plug, simply turn the reel handle forward and the line will start winding in. Practice these movements until you can release and stop the line two or three times before the plug hits the ground.

Once you feel confident with the reel and line control, start to practice cast. Pick out a spot forty or fifty feet away that is clear of trees and bushes. A lawn makes an ideal practice area when water is not available. Never practice on a rough surface that might scuff the line. With the rod at 9:00 in casting position, depress and hold down the push button. Swing the rod tip quickly, with a wrist and forearm motion, to 1:00, elbow close to the body. Then without any hesitation, bring it back to 10:00, re-

Correct way to hold rod and reel when preparing to cast. Reel at 9:00, thumb on push button and handle up.

A. Start cast at 9:00 position, with handle up and push button depressed. B. Swing rod tip to 1:00 with a quick parallel motion. C. Bring rod tip back to 10:00. Release push button allowing line and lure to shoot out toward target. Note: Casting sequence A to B to C is done in one fast continuous motion.

lease the push button, and the plug will shoot out toward the target. You have just made your first cast.

To retrieve the plug, switch the rod to your left hand, palm the reel, and turn the handle with your right hand. Retrieving in this manner lets you "work" the lure and allows better rod leverage when hooked into a large fish. Uniform line tension is also maintained as the line passes between your thumb and forefinger.

A few problems new spin casters encounter and the solutions:

1. High looping casts: occur when the push button is released before the rod tip is back to 10:00, usually between 10:30 and 11:30. This allows the lure and line to shoot up rather than out towards the target.

2. Short, bulletlike casts: occur when the push button is released late and the rod tip is brought down below 9:00. In this position the rod is pointing down into the water and the late release forces the lure down with a heavy splash.

3. Failure to reach the target: usually indicates the rod does not have enough bend to "shoot" the lure out. To get more distance bring the rod tip from 9:00 to 1:00 then back to 10:00 faster, without any hesitation. This will put greater rod bend in the backcast which will give more power on the forward cast. Should this fail, check for tackle balance. The line might be too heavy or the lure too light.

4. Overshooting the target: is usually caused by overpowering the cast. For less distance simply reduce the amount of bend in the rod, just the oppo-

To retrieve plug, switch rod to left hand and palm reel. Turn reel handle forward with right hand.

site of the procedure in #3, or press the reel button to stop the line when the lure is over the target. Practice both these methods, each can be helpful under certain conditions.

5. Line twisting: is usually caused by lures that spin in only one direction. Correct, by using a swivel on the leader. Should a line become badly twisted, remove the lure, pull out all the twisted line so it lies in a straight line, then retrieve in the normal manner.

6. Line does not retrieve when reel handle is turned: is usually caused by slack line or loose coils on the spool. Correct it by lifting the rod tip just as you start to retrieve. If this doesn't work, check the line. It may be too heavy or hard for your size reel.

Side Arm Cast for Spin Casting

Occasionally low hanging trees or bushes will make normal overhand casts impossible. In such cases, use the side arm cast. Everything is done just the same as in a regular cast, except the rod is moved parallel to the water. Rod movement goes from 9:00 to 1:00 back to 10:00 on a clock face parallel, rather than perpendicular, to the water.

If the lure shoots wide, to the left, of the target,

make the correction by releasing the reel button a little sooner, about 10:30 or 11:00.

How to Cast Spinning Tackle

Spinning is the most popular method of casting in America today. The reason being, it can be learned quickly and is used in all types of fishing. This lets the average angler go after all kinds of fish without having to learn three or four casting methods. The

Side arm cast is made with rod parallel to water or ground. Swing rod tip from 9:00 to 1:00 to 10:00 in one fast continuous motion.

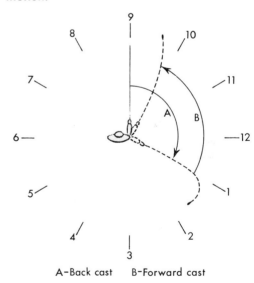

A—Back cast   B—Forward cast

Spinning reel has an open spool and hangs below rod while casting.

Line must be threaded up behind pick-up bait.

casting procedure used in spinning is similar to spin-casting, the only difference being reel manipulation. Unlike the closed faced spin cast reel a spinning reel has an open face and hangs below the rod rather than on top. This gives better casting distance because there is less line friction, and puts the line parallel to the rod guides. This in turn prevents the line from slapping the rod, and gives better rod balance.

Assemble your spinning tackle as follows: Fasten the reel on the reel seat. If sliding lock rings are used, position the reel about ⅔ up the handle in line with the rod guides. Slip the anti-reverse lever to off, pull some line from the spool and thread the rod. Just make sure the line leaves the spool on the inside of the automatic pickup bail. Otherwise, when casting, the line will be down behind the bail. When threaded, reset the anti-reverse lever and tie on a practice plug. The anti-reverse lever stops the handle from turning backwards. Until you can "work" the reel instinctively, it is a good idea to keep the anti-reverse lever on, except to let out line manually.

When assembled, reel in the plug until it hangs six or eight inches from the rod tip and the reel's roller guide is up next to the rod. Grasp the handle so the reel stem is between your second and third finger, and your thumb is along the top. Point the rod tip to 9:00, reach down with your forefinger and pick up

Correct way to hold rod, reel and line when preparing to cast. Rod at 9:00, reel hanging, line locked against rod handle with forefinger.

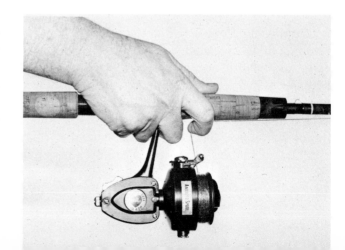

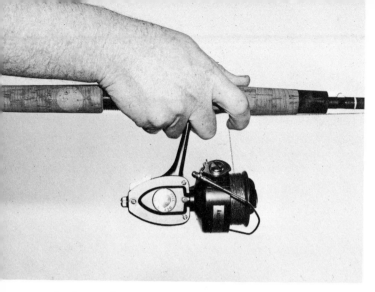

In the ready to cast position, reach over with left hand and snap open pick-up bail by pushing it out and down. The line is now free to shoot out when released.

the line, hold it against the handle, then snap open the pickup bail by pushing it out and down. You are now ready to cast. Before your first cast, however, take a few minutes to get acquainted with the reel and its operation.

With the rod in the 9:00 position ready to cast, drop your forefinger and the plug will fall to the ground. To slow down or stop the plug, brake the line by pressing your forefinger against the side of the spoon. A gentle pressure slows the line down, a firm pressure stops it. To retrieve the plug simply turn the handle in a forward direction with your free hand, and the automatic pickup bail will flip up and

start winding in line. Practice reel control and line "feathering" at the 9:00 position until each move comes easy. If while practicing the line won't spin off, just lower the rod a bit to about 8:30.

When you feel ready, as with spin casting, pick a target forty or fifty feet away that is clear of low hanging trees and bushes. Here, too, a lawn makes a good practice area when water is too far away. Just be careful not to scuff or cut the line when retrieving. Face the target, holding the rod at 9:00 ready to cast. Swing the tip up with a quick wrist and forearm motion to 12:00, elbow close to the body. Then without any hesitation bring the tip back to 10:00, release the line, and the plug will shoot out towards the target. You have just made your first cast. To retrieve the plug, turn the reel handle forward with

Slow or stop the outgoing line by pressing your forefinger against the spool. A gentle pressure slows the line, a firm pressure stops the line. Note the open bail which allows the line to "shoot" free.

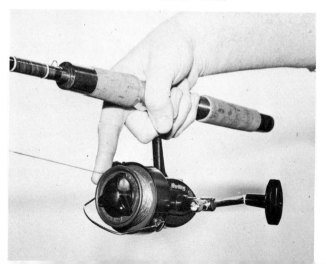

A. Start cast at 9:00 position. Line locked against handle and bail open. B. Swing rod tip to 12:00 in a quick parallel movement. C. Bring rod tip back to 10:00 and release line. Lure will shoot out toward target. Note: Casting sequence A to B to C is done in one fast continuous motion.

your left hand. Southpaws using a left-hand reel would, of course, reel in with their right hand. Practice casting until you are "popping" the target every time. Then go after the big ones.

Some of the problems encountered in spinning and the solutions:

1. High looping casts happen when the line is released before the rod tip gets back to 10:00. An early release, between 10:30 and 11:00, shoots the lure up rather than out towards the target.

2. Short bulletlike casts happen when the line is released late and the rod tip is pointing down into the water, usually between 8:00 or 8:30. This forces the lure down into the water with a loud splash.

3. Failure to reach the target usually indicates that the rod does not have enough bend on the back cast. Bring the rod tip from 9:00 to 12:00 back to 10:00 faster. This will give more power on the forward cast. Should this fail, check for tackle balance. Chances are the line is too heavy or the lure too light.

4. Overshooting the target is usually caused by overpowering the cast. For less distance simply reduce the amount of rod bend or "feather" the line with your forefinger. "Feathering" is especially im-

Loose coils of line may jump from the spool causing a bird's nest if the line is not retrieved under a slight tension.

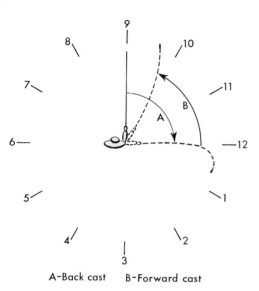

9
8
10
7
11
B
A
6
12
5
1
4
2
3

A-Back cast   B-Forward cast

Side arm cast is made with rod parallel to ground or water. Swing rod tip from 9:00 to 12:00 to 10:00 in one fast continuous motion.

7. Coils of line fall behind the reel's rotating head: is also caused by slack line. Occasionally, after a cast, a few coils fail to shoot through the first guide and fall back behind the rotating head. This usually happens when the rod tip is pointing too high (above 10:00). To prevent this from happening, let the rod tip drift down to about 9:30 after you release the line.

8. Line lies in the water in coils after a cast: most often happens during the first few casts of the day. This is called set and is caused from storing the line on the spool. It will disappear after a few casts. If it does not, chances are your line is too hard. Use a softer (limp) monofilament.

Side Arm Cast for Spinning

When overhanging trees or bushes make it impossible to overhand cast, use the side arm cast. Everything is done the same way except the rod moves parallel to the water. Rod movement goes from 9:00 to 12:00 back to 10:00. If the plug shoots wide, to the left of the target, make the correction by releasing the line sooner, about 10:30 or 11:00, and let the rod drift across to 9:00.

How to Bait Cast

Bait casting, also called plug casting, is as American as catfish, and for many years was the only way to cast a weighted lure in the United States and Canada. Spinning and Spin Casting have, of course, changed all this and now share the spotlight. Sur-

portant when casting and should be practiced until it becomes instinctive.

5. Line Twist is commonly caused by lures that spin, or when the drag clutch is turning while retrieving. The latter usually happens when a large fish is running. Wait until he stops or is moving towards you before retrieving line. If the fault is a spinning lure, use a swivel on the leader.

6. Loose coils of line jumping off the spool is most often the result of slack line and can cause a bird's nest on the spool or at the first line guide. Solve this problem by putting tension on the line when retrieving.

Bring line off spool out through level wind arm before threading rod guides.

prisingly, however, they have not, as some experts predicted, made bait casting obsolete. In fact, even with this competition, it remains one of our most popular methods of fishing, especially among experienced anglers. They learned early in their apprenticeship that bait casting tackle is still the best way to toss big lures (½ to 1 oz.) with pin-point accuracy into weed beds or along stumps where the tackle breaking "lunkers" hide. They also realize that fighting one of these lunkers in his own backyard calls for tackle built to take a beating.

Although bait casting is not recommended for the occasional angler because it takes longer to learn, all young fishermen should master it. Along with becoming a better fisherman, the satisfaction and pride of knowing how is well worth the extra time and effort. Begin by assembling your tackle, including a practice plug (weighted to the rod). Be sure the line passes through the level wind arm before threading the rod guides. When assembled, push the "click" button to "on" and wind in the plug until it is about six inches from the rod tip. Then grip the handle in

your right hand so your thumb rests against the spool and forefinger is around the handle trigger. Point the rod to 9:00, push the "click" button to "off", and turn your wrist until the reel handle is on top (bottom for left-handers). Before casting, however, take a few minutes to practice reel and line control. From the 9:00 position lift your thumb and the spool will start revolving as the plug falls, pulling out line. When the plug hits the ground, chances are the spool will keep turning and cause the line to tangle. This is called a "backlash" and will happen every time the spool overruns (moves faster than) the line or continues to revolve after the lure lands. To prevent backlashing, use your thumb as a brake. To see how this works, reel in the line and let the plug fall again. Only this time keep a very slight thumb pressure on the spool while the plug is falling. Then just as it hits the ground, press down with your thumb and stop the spool. Sound simple? Actually it is, once you develop an "educated" thumb. While learning, however, take advantage of the spool adjustment feature found on all bait casting reels. In the center of the left or right side plate, there is a knurled knob that

Correct way to hold rod, reel and line when preparing to cast. Rod at 9:00, reel handle up, thumb resting against line.

Backlash is caused when the spool revolves faster than the outgoing line or the spool is allowed to revolve after the lure lands. To prevent backlash, control the spool speed with your thumb.

tightens the spool when turned clockwise and loosens it when turned anticlockwise. Tighten this knob until, when the line is released, the plug falls very slowly and the spool stops as the plug hits the ground. This "second" thumb will help prevent backlashing but should be eliminated once your thumb control improves as the added friction reduces casting distance. If backlashing still occurs when you start casting, tighten the drag knob a bit more. The important skill to master is thumb control. Distance can come later.

When you feel ready, pick a clearing free of overhanging trees or bushes, and place a target (newspaper, hula hoop, etc.) about thirty feet away. A lawn makes a good practice area. Avoid any rough surface that might scuff or cut the line. Face the target and point the rod to 9:00, ready to cast. Swing the tip up with a quick wrist and forearm motion to 1:00, elbow close to your body. Then, without any

hesitation, bring the tip back to 10:00 and release the line. As the plug shoots out towards the target, use light thumb pressure to keep the spool and line synchronized. Stop the spool when the plug is over the target. You have just made your first cast. To retrieve the plug, switch the rod to your left hand, palm the reel and turn the handle with your right hand. Retrieving in this manner lets you "work" the lure for better action and allows better rod leverage when hooked onto a large fish. Uniform tension can also be maintained as the line passes between your thumb and forefinger. This ensures even line spooling, necessary to accurate casting.

Free spool reels that allow the spool to revolve without any handle or gear movement are becoming

To prevent backlash while learning to cast, tighten spool with drag clutch knob A.

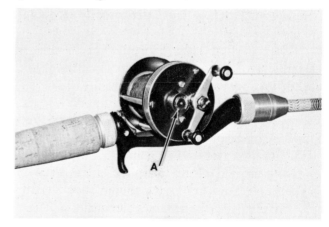

29

A. Start cast at 9:00 position, reel handle up, thumb against line. B. Swing rod tip to 1:00 in a quick parallel movement. C. Bring rod tip back to 10:00 and release line. Lure will shoot out toward target.

more popular among bait casters. Casting with these reels is done exactly the same way as with a conventional reel, the only difference being, before casting, reach over with your left hand and engage the free spool lever.

Some problems new bait casters usually encounter and the solutions:

1. High looping casts: happen when the line is released early, around 10:30 or 11:00, causing the lure to shoot up rather than out towards the target. Wait until 10:00 before lifting your thumb.

2. Short splashing casts: happen when the rod tip is brought below 9:00 and the line released late. In this position, the rod is pointed down into the water and the late release forces the lure down with a loud splash. Start to lift your thumb about 10:15.

3. Failure to reach the target can mean: a. There is too much drag on the anti-backlash knob. Correct by loosening the knob. b. You are not putting enough power into the casting motion. Correct by moving the rod tip faster through the casting arc (9:00 to 1:00 back to 10:00). c. The tackle is not balanced. Check to see if the line is too heavy or lures too light.

4. Overshooting the target indicates you are overpowering the cast. For less distance, simply reduce the amount of rod bend or use your thumb to slow down the spool. Overshooting is desirable when you want the lure to drop on the target area. In such cases, stop the spool by thumbing when the lure passes over the target.

5. Line twist is usually caused by a rotating lure. Put a swivel on the leader.

6. Loose coils of line on the spool happen when the line is retrieved without uniform tension. Use your thumb and forefinger to keep an even pressure on the line as it goes on the spool.

Side Arm Cast for Bait Casting

When overhanging trees or bushes make an overhand cast impossible, use a side arm cast. Everything is done just the same except the rod moves parallel to the water rather than your body and you stand in the center of the clock face. Rod movement goes from 9:00 to 1:00 back to 10:00. If the lure shoots wide, to the left of the target, correct it by releasing the line at 10:30 to 11:00 and let the rod drift across to 9:00.

How to Fly Cast

Fly fishing is, in a sense, the final step for the angler who wants the ultimate in sport fishing. No other method of fishing can match it for thrills, excitement, or satisfaction. Small pan fish, normally landed with ease, become fighting jumping jacks, while larger game fish turn into sky dancing acrobats. Even salt water giants, once the private property of the heavy "hardware" trollers, are now fair prey for the fly enthusiast. So, if after learning to spin or bait cast, you want a bigger challenge and more fun, try fly casting. Fortunately, thanks to today's well-made and balanced tackle, fly casting is easy to master.

Most problems encountered by new fly fishermen develop from unbalanced tackle. Usually the line which supplies the weight to cast weightless flies, streamers, etc., is too light or heavy for the rod. This spoils natural rod action, making accurate casting

To retrieve the lure, switch rod to left hand, palm the reel and turn handle with your right hand. While retrieving, let the line slide between your thumb and forefinger. This keeps an even tension on the spooled line, cleans off any dirt, and points up any cuts or breaks.

Side arm cast is made with rod parallel to ground or water. Swing rod tip from 9:00 to 1:00 to 10:00 in one fast continuous motion.

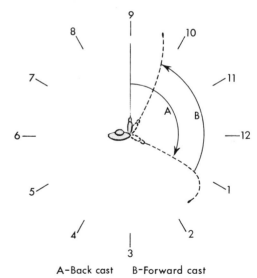

A–Back cast   B–Forward cast

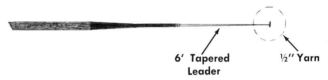

Use a short tapered leader and a ½ inch piece of yarn while practice casting.

impossible. So before you start practicing, be sure to read, "How to Select Your Equipment" on page 11 and "How to Balance Equipment" on page 14. This information will make learning easier and will get you out over fish much sooner.

While assembling your tackle, be extra careful that rod guides are in line and the fly line, if it is a weight forward taper, has the heavy section up front. Plan also, while practicing, to use a six-foot tapered leader with a half-inch piece of bright colored yarn tied to the tip. The short leader is easier to cast and the yarn will act as a hookless fly. Later as your casting technique improves, work up to 7½ to 9 foot leaders with tippets and larger flies or streamers. Figure 6, page 11 shows how to attach the leader to the line, tippet to leader, and fly to tippet.

After the tackle is assembled, take a few minutes to get acquainted with the feel and action of the rod. Hold it in the right hand with the reel hanging down and your grip just forward of the reel with thumb on top. Southpaws would use their left hand.

A "Trophy" for Mike.

Correct way to hold rod and reel. Hand in front of reel which hangs below the rod.

When ready to cast, pick out a smooth-cut grass clearing at least 100 feet long. The smooth-cut grass will protect your expensive line from getting scuffed. Walk to the center of the practice area, strip twenty-five to thirty feet of fly line from the reel, lay the rod down and stretch the line straight out on the grass. A "'target" can easily be laid out by placing a hoop or piece of paper under the colored yarn. In this position, the line is ready to back cast and twenty-five to thirty feet has proven the best practice distance to begin casting. Thirty feet plus the rod length will also reach most fishing spots. So don't worry about distance; later, when your "tossing" is easy, will be time enough.

With the line stretched out, pick up the rod with your right hand, point the tip to 9:00 and keep your elbow close to the body. Then reach over and take the line in your left hand about halfway between the

reel and first guide. Now, instead of squarely facing the target, as in other methods of casting, turn your body about 45 degrees to the right, but keep the rod tip pointing at the target. This lets you watch the line during the back cast. Later, when you develop the right timing, turn and face the target. To start the cast, slowly move your right arm forward about three or four inches and pull in any slack line with the left hand. Then, with a smooth but rapid movement, raise the rod tip to 12:00 using a forearm and elbow action only. If done properly the line will be airborne by 11:00, passing above and behind the rod tip in a shallow U-shaped loop. As the line passes overhead, let your right shoulder drift backwards a few inches and watch the loop start to straighten out. The moment the line and leader are

While learning to cast, hold the rod on target, but turn your body 45° to right. This lets you watch the line during the back cast. Once you develop the right timing, face the target as in other methods of casting.

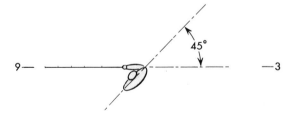

A. Start the cast at 9:00 position with right arm forward 3 or 4 inches. Hold slack line in left hand. Turn your body 45° to right while learning. B. Raise rod tip in a smooth rapid forearm motion to 12:00. As the line moves overhead let your right shoulder drift back a few inches and watch the line straighten out. C. The moment the line and leader are fully extended, make smooth rapid forward cast to 10:00. If done properly, the line will shoot out until fully extended and the fly will settle gently on the target.

fully extended, start the forward cast. Bring your shoulder back to its starting position while driving the rod forward to 10:00 with a forearm and elbow motion. The line and leader will shoot ahead in a tight U-loop, slowly straightening out until the fly gently settles on the target. During both the back and forward cast, your wrist remains rigid and the line is held tightly in the left hand.

If your first few casts fail to perform properly, don't get discouraged; keep practicing, a few minutes at a time, until your timing and line control is perfected. Hurrying the cast is the most common fault of beginners. While this may be proper in spin and bait casting, fly casting calls for a short hesitation at 12:00 to let the line straighten out. So wait until the exact moment the line is fully extended and you feel a slight "tug" before starting the forward cast. Failure to wait will cause the line to crack like a whip and probably snap the fly off. While on the other hand if you wait too long and the line starts back before the forward cast is begun, it will fall to

Wait until line is fully extended and you feel a slight "tug" before starting the forward cast.

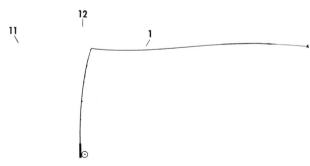

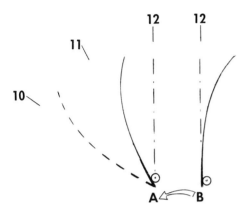

To correct weak forward casts, rod or line hooking, or wind knots use more power. Drive the rod forward in a 12:00 position until your right shoulder is back to its starting position B to A. Then power the rod tip to 11:00 and on to 10:00.

the ground or down over your head. This can also happen if you flex your wrist during the cast.

Some tips to help correct other common casting faults are:

1. Line won't straighten out on back or forward cast: is usually an indication that you are waving the rod through the casting arc with wrist action, or line is slipping through the guides. Correct by keeping your wrist rigid throughout the casting arc and hold the line tightly in your left hand.

2. Line hits the ground on back cast: happens when the rod tip moves to 2:00 or 3:00 on the back cast. Correct by stopping at 12:00 and keep your wrist rigid.

3. Hooking the line with the fly: happens when the rod tip is dropped too soon on the forward cast. Correct by bringing the rod tip forward in a 12:00 position until your forearm is pointing to 11:00. Then let the rod tip drop to 10:00 as the forearm moves down. This is the natural casting arc and should be done without flexing the wrist.

4. Fly drops below line on the forward cast: Cause and correction are the same as Hooking the Line.

5. Fly hits the rod: Cause and correction same as Hooking the Line.

6. Wind knots: (knots form on the leader while casting): Cause and correction the same as Hooking the Line.

7. Fly, leader and line splashes on water: happens when the forward cast is aimed too low. Correction: Don't let rod tip drop below 10:00 and aim the fly three or four feet above the target, allowing it to settle gently on the water.

Note: When casting into a wind it may be necessary to power cast the rod to 9:00 allowing the line to "shoot" under the wind force. Do not, however, attempt this while learning the basic overhand cast.

8. Line and leader piled up at end of cast: happens when, 1. Not enough power is put into forward cast. 2. Rod tip is dropped too soon on forward cast.

During back cast, lock line against rod with right forefinger and strip line from reel with left hand.

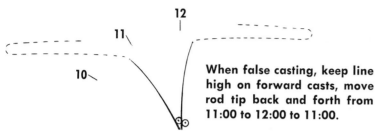

12

11

10

When false casting, keep line high on forward casts, move rod tip back and forth from 11:00 to 12:00 to 11:00.

3. A combination of not enough power and dropping tip. 4. Line is released too soon when shooting for distance (see False Casting).

False Casting

Once you can "throw" with some degree of accuracy it is time to learn false casting, which means making two or more consecutive casts without the fly touching the water. This eliminates the need of laying out line each time you start a new cast, and makes possible added distance when needed. False casting also lets you change casting direction or dry a floating fly that becomes waterlogged.

Begin by stripping line off the reel until twelve to fifteen feet hang from the rod tip. Then, holding the rod in a 9:00 casting position, make a regular back cast to 12:00. Wait for the line to straighten out, then start a normal forward cast but stop at 11:00 or 10:30 instead of 10:00. This will keep the line higher off the water, giving you more time to recover. Once the line is straightened out, start the

back cast immediately. Repeat this casting cycle three or four times in succession, bearing in mind the timing and hesitation are the same for both back and forward casts, the only difference being, a shorter line has a shorter hesitation.

To get more distance, lock the line against the rod handle with your right forefinger. Then during the back cast, strip three or four feet of line from the reel with your left hand. On the forward cast drop your finger when the rod tip reaches 11:00 and the loose line will shoot up and through the guides. When the line straightens out begin the back cast, lock the line with your right forefinger and strip off another three or four feet of line. Repeat this cycle of lock-strip-cast until you have the necessary amount of line out. Then let the fly settle gently to the water. When done properly the line will shoot back and forth in a series of shallow U-loops getting longer as more line is played out. Any problems you encounter will be similar to those found in the basic overhand cast and are solved in the same way.

When retrieving line, use the reach-pull-coil-lock sequence until only 12 to 15 feet of line remain on the water.

Retrieving

Unlike other methods of fishing, the fly reel is rarely used to retrieve line after a cast, the exception being when bringing in a large fish. The system used instead is similar to line stripping only in reverse. When the fly is on the water, reach up with your left hand, grasp the line just below the butt guide and pull in until your hand is by your waist, holding a loose coil of line. Then lock the line against the rod with your right forefinger. Repeat this action of reach-pull-coil-lock until only twelve to fifteen feet of line remains on the water and you are again ready to cast. Small fish are usually landed this way.

Roll Cast

Another cast every fly fisherman should master is the roll cast, used in areas where back casting is impossible because of bushes, trees or high winds.

Start by stripping twelve to fifteen feet of line from the reel and flipping it with the rod tip out in front of you. Then from a 9:00 position slowly bring the rod tip back to 1:00 and stop. The line should now be hanging in a shallow loop behind and slightly away from your shoulder, extending down onto the water. From this position drive the rod tip down to 10:00 in a fast whipping motion. The line will move forward in a rolling loop until it is fully extended in the same direction the rod is pointed. To get more distance strip another six to eight feet of line from the reel and hold it in your free hand. Repeat the roll cast, releasing the new line when the rod tip is at 10:00. If done right, the new line will be pulled out and roll across the water. Continue this line stripping and casting motion until you have enough distance, usually thirty to forty feet.

Fly Fishing Tips

1. Use only tapered leaders on your fly line. Level leaders make casting much more difficult. A good tapered leader will have the butt end nearly the same diameter as the line it is attached to. (See leaders on Page 12.)

2. Clean your fly line before each fishing trip, using the cleaner supplied with the line or mild soap

A. Correct 1:00 position for roll cast. Notice shallow loop behind fisherman extending down out onto water. B. From 1:00 position, drive rod down to 10:00 in a fast whipping motion. If done correctly, the line will move forward in a large rolling loop until fully extended.

on a damp cloth. Just be extra sure to wipe off all excess cleaner.

3. When casting, work the nearby waters first, gradually reaching out until all likely spots are covered. This method is less likely to "spook" fish with line movement.

4. When casting to a rising fish, never cast into the center of the rise. This will often put a fish "down." Instead, "throw" in front or either side where the fish can still see the fly without becoming alarmed.

5. When a fish strikes, set the hook immediately by snubbing the line against the rod handle with the forefinger of your rod hand. This trick, used by the "pros," gives positive line control.

6. When landing a fish, turn the rod over so the guides and reel are on top. This lets any knots in the leader and tippet slip through the guides easier, should the fish make a final run.

7. Check your leader and tippet often for worn

spots or cuts, always after you land a fish or the line gets snagged.

Salt Water Surf Casting

If you live near the ocean where surf casting is

When casting "work" the nearby waters first, gradually reaching out to include all likely spots.

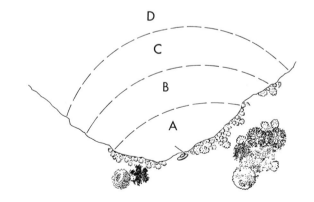

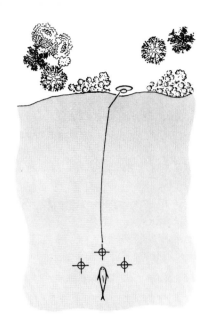

Always cast in front or to either side of a rising fish. This lets the fish see the lure without becoming alarmed.

250 yard minimum, 50 lb. test line capacity. The line should be a good grade nylon, dacron or monofilament in the thirty to eighty pound test class. Hooks, lures and wire leaders should all be corrosion resistant.

Casting is done with two hands because of the size and weight of equipment. Line control is done the same way as with fresh water equipment, using the thumb on bait casting and the forefinger on spinning. Assembling surf tackle is also similar to the procedure of fresh water gear. (Read "How to Bait Cast," Page 27 and "How to Cast Spinning Tackle," Page 23.)

Once your tackle is assembled and you can "work" the reel, pick out a clearing at least 200 feet

While landing a fish, turn the rod over. This allows any knots in the leader to slide through the guides without snagging.

popular, chances are you will become a "surf" addict. The equipment used is similar to bait casting or spinning tackle only much bigger and stronger. This is necessary because the fish you catch can weigh fifty pounds or more. When buying a surf outfit use the same criteria (quality construction and materials plus balance) for selecting fresh water tackle (read "How to Balance Equipment" on Page 16). Surf rods for boys should have a medium action and range between seven and one-half to nine and one-half feet long. Reels should be designed for salt water surf casting and have a

John Salonis with his world record 68½ lb. striped bass caught on 30 lb. test line.

long by 75 feet wide and start to practice cast. Reel in until the practice lure or leader snap is about one foot from the rod tip. Then, assuming you are right-handed (left-handers just the opposite), hold the rod so your right hand controls the reel and your left hand is near the butt (end of handle). Next, stand sideways, with your left shoulder and foot pointing toward the target and your feet spread comfortably apart. Raise the rod tip to 2:00, hold your elbow close to the body, and prepare to cast. Using a fast push-throwing motion with your right hand, swing the rod tip down to 10:00 and release the line. When done properly, the lure will shoot out in a shallow arc straight towards the target. During the cast, your left hand acts as a pivot point for the rod and can be held in the most comfortable position.

To retrieve the lure turn your body so you face the target. Then hold the rod butt (end) against your stomach or in a casting belt, grasp the handle just above the reel with your left hand and reel in with the right hand. Just be sure to keep tension on the line while retrieving.

Once you can "throw" with some accuracy start pivoting your body during the cast, so you end up facing the target. Make the pivot by "swinging" your right leg and shoulder forward in concert with the rod. This is a natural reaction if your left foot is pointed towards the target and will, after a little practice, become automatic. When more distance is needed, a slight push with the right foot and shoul-

Reel control in surf casting is similar to freshwater casting.

der will give added power to the cast.

Some problems usually encountered in surf casting and the solutions:

1. Backlashing (bait casting reel) is caused by poor thumb control. The spool is allowed to turn faster than the outgoing line or the spool keeps turning after the lure is in the water.

2. Line twist is caused by lures or bait that revolve when being retrieved. Correct by using a swivel on the leader. When using a spinning reel line, twist also occurs if you continue to reel in when the drag clutch is slipping.

3. High looping casts are caused when the line is released too early, about 11:00. This allows the line to shoot up rather than out towards the target. Wait until 10:15 or 10:00 before releasing the line.

4. Short splashing casts occur when the rod is

brought down below 9:00 and the line is released late. Correct by releasing line at 10:00.

5. Failure to reach the target area could mean: 1. The tackle is not balanced. Check to see if the line is too heavy or lures too light. 2. You are not putting enough power into the casting motion. Correct

A. Stand sideways with left foot and shoulder pointed at the target. Rod tip at 2:00, right hand on reel, left hand near rod butt, right elbow close to body. B. From the 2:00 position, make a fast push-throw motion with your right hand driving the rod to 10:00. At 10:00 release the line and lure will shoot out.

To retrieve, face the target, brace rod butt against your belt, grasp the handle above the reel, reel in with free hand.

by moving the rod faster through the casting arc, giving more push with the back leg and shoulder.

6. Overshooting the target area indicates too much power during the cast. For less distance, simply reduce power or use line control (thumbing or forefinger).

HOW TO TROLL

Trolling means to pull or tow a lure behind a moving boat. The object is to cover a large area of water and eliminate the need for casting. This method of fishing is especially productive on strange waterways where you have to go looking for the fish.

In areas where trolling is the popular way to fish, you may want to buy trolling equipment (read "Trolling Tackle" on Page 17). If, however, you will only troll occasionally, use your regular tackle. Just be sure it is not too light for the fish you will be catching.

Following are some procedures and tips that will

42

help catch fish and make your outings more enjoyable.

1. The boat or canoe you fish from should be in A-1 condition and have all the required safety equipment.

2. There should be a Coast Guard approved life preserver for each passenger. All non- and poor swimmers should wear their preservers while on board. The yoke type preserver is recommended as the best and easiest to use. DO NOT use the seat cushion type life preserver. In an emergency, they are extremely difficult for nonswimmers to use.

3. Limit the number of lines being trolled to three. One over the transom (back) and one over each side.

4. While trolling, keep each line a different length. Ex: When using three lines, have one about twenty yards long, the second, thirty yards and the third, forty yards. This method of "towing" helps prevent line tangling.

5. Should lines tangle, reel in slowly, clearing them as they come in. Do this while still under way

Once you master rod movement, start swinging your right leg and shoulder forward as you cast from 2:00 to 10:00. This motion gives added power and puts you into the proper retrieve position.

is a good idea to increase speed slightly when turning.

8. Be extra careful when turning or retrieving to keep lines clear of the propeller. Should one get tangled, stop the engine immediately and clear all lines from the prop or propeller shaft.

9. Keep rods in a ready position (between 10:00 and 10:30). Make sure the drag clutch on each reel is set properly. (See "How to Fight and Land a Fish," Page 46.)

Limit number of lines to three and have each a different length.

Troll each line at a different depth until you find what level fish are at.

Trolling with 3 lines

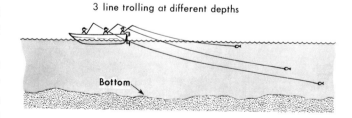

3 line trolling at different depths

Bottom

if you have another line out. Otherwise, stop the boat and keep the engine idling in neutral.

6. When beginning to fish, troll each lure at a different depth. This is the best and quickest way to locate the level at which the fish are feeding. Once you locate this level, adjust the line weights or other lures for the same depth.

7. When turning the boat make wide turns. This keeps the lines spaced evenly apart. Slow narrow turns let lines and lures sink and hang up on the bottom or run over each other causing a tangle. It

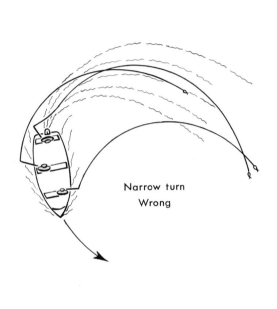

Narrow turn
Wrong

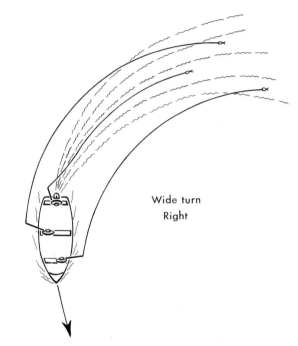

Wide turn
Right

When turning, make wide turns and increase speed slightly.

10. Avoid pulling lines and lures through weed beds. Stay along the edges. When trolling deep or in weed infested waters, check lures and lines occa-sionally. Fish rarely strike lures fouled with vegetation.

11. When fighting and landing a fish, stop the boat and shift the engine to neutral. Sometimes, however, when fighting extra large salt water fish it is necessary to use the boat to follow or turn the fish.

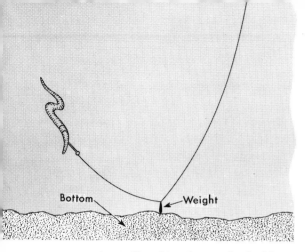

One favorite method of bottom fishing is to place a small weight 6 to 18 inches behind the hook. This holds bait on bottom but allows it to swim or swing free.

STILL FISHING

Another excellent way to catch fish is by still fishing, called dock or bridge fishing in some areas. Just cast, toss or float a baited hook out on the water and let it lie still instead of retrieving. This method is popular with new fishermen because only minimum skills are needed, and when fishing well stocked waters the action is fast and furious.

There are two ways to still fish: on the bottom and at or near the surface with a bobber (float). To bottom fish you place a small weight, six to eighteen inches behind the hook and let the bait sink to the bottom where deep feeding fish lie. The size weight

needed will depend on water currents and buoyancy of the bait, use just enough to hold the bait down.

In bobber fishing a small float, called a bobber, holds the bait on or near the surface where top feeding fish congregate. How deep below the surface the bait hangs is determined by the distance up the line the bobber is attached. A good rule of thumb states: Never have the distance between hook and bobber longer than your fishing pole. This makes casting or landing fish easier.

In both methods of fishing, once the bait is cast or tossed out, retrieve just enough line to take up any slack. Then when a fish strikes you are ready to set the hook. This is especially important when bottom fishing because the only way you know a fish is biting is by feel. In bobber fishing the float bobs un-

Bobber attached to line keeps bait off bottom and bobs up and down or is pulled under when a fish strikes.

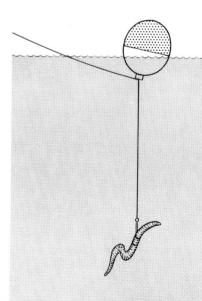

der during a strike but too much slack line prevents setting the hook in time.

Retrieving is done the same as in all other methods of fishing. Hold the rod at a 45 degree angle and reel in fast or slow depending on conditions, the major difference being you only retrieve to check or change the bait and when landing a fish.

Following are a few still fishing tips that will help you catch more fish:

1. Fish up current or wind. In this position the bait and line is prevented from drifting to shore.

2. Change the depth of the bait every fifteen or twenty minutes until you find the right level and start catching fish. Make the depth adjustment by sliding the bobber up or down the line. Just remember not to have the distance between hook and bobber longer than the fishing pole.

3. When bobber fishing in a current, use a small weight, just above the hook, to hold the bait down.

4. When using free swimming live bait (minnows, eels, frogs, etc.), be sure the float is large enough to prevent the bait from pulling it under.

5. When fishing with nonswimming or food bait use a small bobber that just barely floats. This assures an instant response when a fish bites and minimizes any drag when he runs.

HOW TO FIGHT AND LAND A FISH

Most of the thrills in sport fishing come while fighting and landing a fish. These are the times when balanced tackle and know-how pay off, especially if the hooked fish is a potential "tackle buster." With this in mind, read this chapter thoroughly. Then instead of having to tell about the big ones that got away, you will have bragging pictures of the "lunkers" you landed.

Setting the Drag Clutch

Before beginning to fish, set the drag clutch on your reel. Fish with hard bony mouths, need a heavy setting to drive the hook home. Fish with soft, delicate mouths need a light setting to prevent their "pulling" or "wearing" off the hook. In waters where various species are present, set the tension between heavy and light. Never set tension just under the lines' breaking point, except when using ultra light tackle (2 lbs. test or less). This bad habit is a major reason for lost fish.

A simple method for determining tension is to set the hook into a small piece of heavy belt leather or

light buckskin. Both are easily carried in a tackle box or pocket. On a heavy setting the hook point will penetrate up to the barb before the clutch starts slipping. Whereas, on a light setting, the hook will just "bite" through the buckskin before the clutch starts slipping. Settings will also vary with hook size and sharpness. Thick hooks need a heavier setting than thin wire hooks and dull hooks catch only water. So be doubly sure your hooks are needle sharp.

Setting the Hook

Although fish do on occasions hook themselves, the vast majority must be hooked by the fisherman. This is best done by holding the rod at about a 45 degree angle to the water. Then when a fish strikes, give the rod a strong, quick rearward and upward movement keeping the same 45 degree angle. Re-

Rod is held at about 45° to water when setting hook. This angle gives the best leverage and lets all the rod work in a natural bend.

peat the set a second time if the fish is a hard-mouthed specie.

When to set the hook will depend on the kind of bait and fish. If artificial lures or flies are being used, set the hook immediately. If live bait is being used, the time lapse between the strike and setting the hook can be up to ten seconds. A good rule thumb for live baits is: when using small bait (worms, crickets, etc.) that the fish can easily swallow in one bite, set the hook immediately. When using large bait (fish, frogs, etc.), give the fish time to mouth and run with the bait, then swallow it. This can take up to ten seconds, depending on the type fish. Here again is where the advice of an experienced fisherman or a bait dealer can be helpful.

Often fish are lost because the line stretches while setting the hook. To prevent this, especially when a lot of line is out, crank the reel handle while setting the hook.

Playing the Fish

Once your fish is hooked, the battle begins. Try to keep the rod at the same 45 degree angle as when setting the hook. This angle gives the best rod leverage and minimizes the chance of tackle failure. If the fish is strong let him run against the drag tension, but don't reel in while the drag is turning. When there is a current try to keep him up stream, swimming into the current. This takes pressure off the line and tires the fish.

Often, when a fish is trophy size it is difficult to

retrieve line by reeling in. In such cases, pump the rod. Slowly raise the rod tip to 11:00. Then quickly drop it down to 9:30 and quickly reel in the slack line. Repeat this motion until the fish is close enough to land.

When obstructions (weeds, stumps, etc.) are close by, get your fish clear as quickly as possible. If he stops to rest and is too heavy to reel in, tap the rod butt with your hand or twang the line like a guitar string. This will usually start him moving again.

Jumpers need special handling. When using a weighted lure (plug, spoon or spinner), keep the line tight during the jump. A slack line at this time will let the fish throw the lure. If, however, the lure is unweighted (flies, streamers, etc.), attached to a light leader, it is best to drop the rod tip and give slack line during the jumps. This prevents the fish from breaking the leader if he falls back on the line.

Landing the Fish

Small fish rarely give any trouble while being landed. Just draw them into your net or hand and lift from the water. See Figure 51 on page 39.

A large fish, however, needs special care. Make sure they are tired before leading them to net or gaff. Tired fish roll on their side and offer minimum resistance. Try to keep the rod angle at 45 degrees, about 10:30. Don't make the mistake of holding it at 12:00 or 1:00. In these positions, a large fish can easily break the line or rod tip. And most im-

portant, stay alert for a sudden dash to freedom. This usually occurs when a fish first sees the fisherman, net, or boat. When this happens release the line and let the fish run. After he stops, begin again to retrieve and land.

Releasing the Fish

Unless you plan to eat or mount your fish, make a habit of releasing them. This conservation practice is becoming more and more popular among real sport fishermen, the theory being, that every fish put back means another fish to catch.

The easiest way to release a fish is to reach down in the water and twist the hook from its mouth. On soft-mouthed fish, just a simple twist will do. With hard-mouthed or sharp-toothed fish, let a pair of pliers substitute for your fingers. In cases where the hook has been swallowed, cut the leader as close to the hook as possible.

When a photograph is wanted, lift the fish from the water by gill or the tail, snap the picture, then release him. Use a heavy leather work glove when handling sharp-toothed fish.

FAVORITE LURES AND BAITS

Over the years, thousands of different lures and baits have caught fish. Of these a certain few have become favorites by attracting fish year after year.

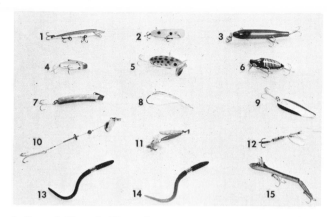

1. Normark "Rappala Minnow"
2. Helin "Flatfish"
3. Creek Chub "Pikie Minnow"
4. Heddon "Super Sonic"
5. Arbogast "Jitterbug"
6. Heddon "River Runt"
7. South Bend "Super Duper"
8. Johnson "Silver Spoon"
9. Eppinger "Dardevle"
10. "Minnow Rig Spinner"
11. Garcia "Abu Reflex"
12. Heddon "Hep Spinner"
13. Plastic Worm (Black)
14. Plastic Worm (Natural)
15. French "Eelet"

As a new fisherman, select your first lures and baits from these classics. Later, when you have a better understanding of fish habits, you can experiment with new designs and feeds.

Fresh Water

Lures—Following are fifteen proven artificial lures (6 plugs, 3 spoons, 3 spinners, 2 plastic worms and an eel) that meet just about any fishing condition. They come in various sizes and colors, and are made for all methods of fishing. What size to use is best determined by the average size of the fish you will be catching. A general rule of thumb states: small and medium size lures catch big and small fish, while large lures catch only large fish. Color is not important except that dark lures seem to catch more fish on overcast days and at night. More important than color is finding what level the fish are swimming and "working" the lures, as explained in the directions, at that depth.

Surface Lures—Float and stay on the surface while being "worked" during the retrieve. This makes them an excellent choice around and over shallow weed beds, lily pads, stumps, etc. A slow retrieve with occasional jerks or "pops" and frequent stops to let the lure lie still usually produce the best catches. Don't be afraid, however, to break the rule occasionally, and "skitter" the lure across the water with a fast retrieve. This reverse psychology sometimes riles up a "lunker" into striking.

Shallow Running Lures—Float at rest but dive and "swim" at various depths down to ten feet depending on the rate of retrieve. The faster the retrieve the deeper the lure "swims." Work these lures the same as floating lures only add a few variations to get some wiggling actions.

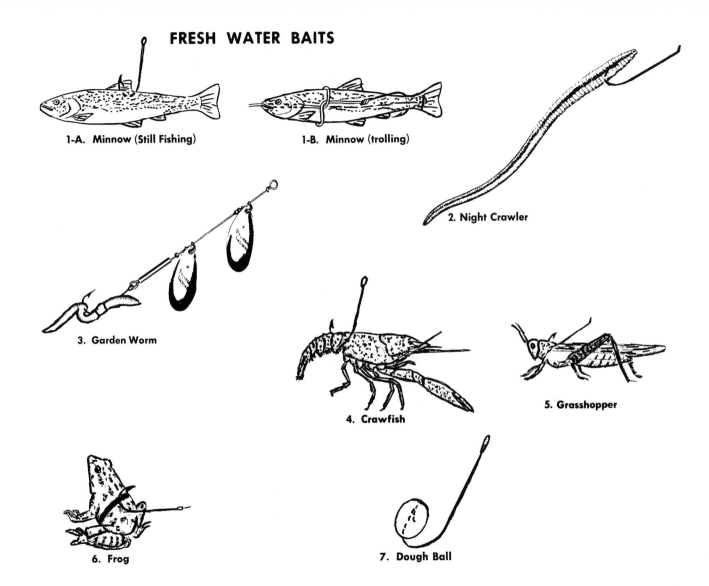

FRESH WATER BAITS

1-A. Minnow (Still Fishing)

1-B. Minnow (trolling)

2. Night Crawler

3. Garden Worm

4. Crawfish

5. Grasshopper

6. Frog

7. Dough Ball

1 (A-B). Minnows are the general name given most small fish used for bait (shiners, chubs, hard-heads). They are also the most popular live bait for all game fish above pan fish size. 1-A shows the approved way to rig a minnow for still fishing. Run the hook just under the tough skin along the dorsal fin. During a strike, let the fish run and swallow the bait before setting the hook. 1-B shows a trolling and casting rig with a dead minnow. Run the hook or line through the mouth and out a gill opening. Then loop the line just in front of the dorsal fin, set the hook into the fleshy part of the tail and draw the line up snug.

Use a minnow pail to keep the bait alive while fishing.

2. Night Crawlers are the giants of the worm family, growing up to one foot long. When used singly or in "a gob" (two or more), they are excellent big bass and trout bait. When cut up in small pieces, they make good pan fish bait. Fig. 65 #2 shows a casting or trolling rig. For still fishing, hook them in two or three places as shown in #3. Just make sure you leave plenty of tail to wiggle. Set the hook fast when you get a strike.

Store worms in a well-ventilated container that has a mixture of earth and damp grass or leaves.

3. Garden Worms are the small angle worms, two to three inches long, we dig up in the garden. Hook and fish them the same as night crawlers only use smaller hooks. Most anglers who enjoy pan fishing prefer garden worms because they are much livelier than night crawlers and can be used whole. Keep them in a well-ventilated can or small box that has a mixture of dirt and damp grass or leaves.

4. Crawfish are tiny fresh water lobsters, one to three inches long, and are a favorite bass food. Look for them in shallow water under rocks and sunken logs. Be careful when picking them up or the front claws will nip you. Crawfish are hooked through the tail and still fished with a bobber. This keeps them off the bottom where they would quickly crawl under a rock, safe from any hungry bass. During a strike, wait until the fish has a chance to run and swallow the bait before setting the hook.

Crawfish are best kept in a bait bucket half filled with water or a container lined with wet grass or moss.

5. Grasshoppers make excellent trout, bass and pan fish bait, especially when the stream or lake you are fishing borders a grassy field or meadow, where grasshoppers are in good supply. Put the hook lightly through the neck collar and let them float on the surface without any bobber as if they had hopped or fallen into the water. The strike will come fast as in dry fly fishing so be ready to set the hook quickly. Keep grasshoppers in a grass-lined plastic jar with a screw cap top. Punch a few air holes in the cap for ventilation. Don't use a glass jar as it can be dangerous if broken.

6. Frogs are sure-fire baits for northern pike, pickerel, and muskellunge as well as large trout and the bass family. Hook them through the upper lip (never both lips or they will drown) or with a special frog harness. #6 shows a simple elastic band harness. Still fish a frog without any weight or bobber so it can swim free. Just be careful it doesn't swim into a weed bed or lily pads that would let a striking fish foul the line. During

a strike, let the fish run, then swallow the frog before setting the hook.

Catch frogs in and around shallow weed beds and lily pads with a small net. Use a net bag (about the size of a small onion sack) lined with damp grass or seaweed to keep your frogs.

7. Dough Balls in one form or another are probably the most popular pan fish bait in the world. Made from fresh bread or biscuit dough or moistened white bread, you roll a small piece into a ball and place it on the tip of a hook. The size of the ball is determined by hook size. Still fish dough balls with either a bobber or on the bottom. Be ready to set the hook fast as pan fish tend to nibble bait rather than run and swallow it. The trick is to catch them nibbling.

Keep the dough moist in a plastic bag by adding a little water occasionally.

Deep Running Lures—Include all spoons, spinners, and sinking plugs. These lures can be fished at any depth by regulating the speed of retrieve or trolling. The slower the retrieve, the deeper the lure will "swim." Although many spoons and spinners make excellent shallow water lures by fast retrieving, they perform best when you must go down deep after the lunkers.

Baits—Long before artificial lures were invented, live and food baits were catching fish. And like the artificials, certain baits have become favorites. Following are seven top baits, telling how to attach the hook and fish them.

Flies, Nymphs and Streamers—Fly casters are constantly experimenting with new artificials but like all fishermen they turn to old standbys when fish refuse to cooperate. Following are the more popular types and a few recommended patterns. Hook size depends on type and size of fish.

Dry Flies imitate live flying insects that have just hatched or fallen on the surface. Presented correctly, a "dry" is cast up and across stream. On the downstream drift it must float free, without any drag or pull from line or leader. Even the slightest variation from a natural float will alert trout or salmon. This perfection calls for lots of practice and can at times become frustrating. To avoid getting discouraged practice on pan fish (Sunnies, Blue Gills, Crappies, etc.). They are always hungry and will overlook a few casting mistakes while providing a world of fun. Once you feel confident, and can set a hook automatically on a strike, head for trout or salmon waters.

Wet Flies imitate flying insects that, after falling on the water, have sunk below the surface and are being swept downstream. Present a "wet" the same way you work a dry fly. Cast up and across stream to get a natural drift without any line or leader drag. Set the hook instantly on a strike.

Nymphs imitate the larva stage of aquatic insects and should be fished as such. Some natural nymphs crawl around the bottom, others float just below the surface preparing to emerge on the surface as flying insects.

In quiet waters, artificials that represent crawling

VARIETIES OF FLIES

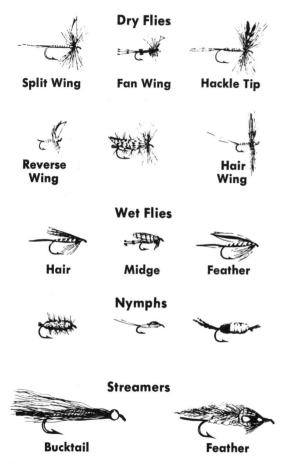

Dry Flies

Split Wing   **Fan Wing**   **Hackle Tip**

Reverse Wing   **Hair Wing**

Wet Flies

Hair   **Midge**   **Feather**

Nymphs

Streamers

Bucktail   **Feather**

Various types of flies, nymphs and streamers.

or swimming nymphs should be worked along the bottom in series of twitches and repeated pauses. In fast currents, let them tumble along the bottom as if fishing a natural.

"Work" floating nymphs as you do dry or wet flies. Concentrate on a good float and a fast hook set during a strike.

Streamers imitate minnows and other bait fish. One favorite method of working streamers is to let them sink in quiet waters or drift submerged downstream. Then retrieve in a series of short jerks and slow even pulls of about three feet. When done correctly, the streamer will act like a bait fish slowly cruising along with short erratic darts after food. Learn how to fish streamers, or any other fly, by watching the actions of natural bait, then practice until you can imitate their movements.

Salt Water

Salt water fishing also has its classic lures and baits. The lures, developed for ocean use, are similar but bigger than their fresh water counterparts, and the better made models will be rust and corrosion resistant.

Following are a few of the more popular salt water baits with information on how to fish them.

SALT WATER BAITS

1. Rigged Eel (Trolling-Casting)

2. Blood and Sand Worm

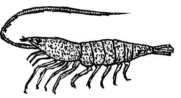

5. Shrimp

3. Squid

6. Baitfish

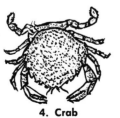

4. Crab

7. Clam

1. Rigged Eels are one of the top baits for striped bass on the Northeastern and West Coast. When using whole eels, thread them with stainless wire or light ball chain and have two hooks attached as shown in Fig. 69 #1. Empty eel skins are also used with a special weighed head for deep fishing. Eels produce best results when trolled or surf cast.

2. Blood and Sand Worms enjoy the same universal appeal among salt water fish that their land cousins have with fresh water fish. Rig them whole either singular or in a gob (two or more) for large fish. On small fish, use a small piece of worm placed on the end of your hook. Sea worms can be trolled, cast or still fished. All methods produce equally well if fish are "in."

3. Squid, six to twelve inches long, are a favorite bait along the northeastern seaboard for many species of game fish. When used whole, rig them with the hook embedded in the head allowing the "tails" (arms) to move freely. Squid produce best when surf casting or trolling. In both methods, jerk the rod while retrieving or pulling so the bait looks alive. Pieces of squid cut up into chunks make good bait when still fishing on the bottom.

4. Crabs are used on all coasts to catch many species of salt water game fish. When used whole, rig the hook through the back, under the top shell and out the bottom shell. If the crab is a soft shell (growing a new shell) or cut up into pieces use a rubber band rig, similar to a frog rig in fresh water fishing. Still fishing is the most productive way to fish crabs. Floating a whole crab without a bobber over a feeding area, will also produce excellent results when conditions are right. Keep your crabs in a ventilated container lined with seaweed.

5. Shrimp are the basic diet for many salt water game fish and for this reason make an excellent bait. Rig them through the tail so the hook is completely covered up to the shank. Still fishing, floating and slow trolling produce the best results. Use two or more shrimp on a hook when fishing for large game fish. Keep your shrimp in a ventilated box lined with wet seaweed.

6. Bait Fish include dozens of different species. A few of the more common are: herring, smelts, mullet, mackerel, killifish, sand eels, and menhaden. All salt water bait fish can be rigged and fished the same as their fresh water cousins. For still fishing rig the hook just under the dorsal fin. When trolling, use the threaded trolling rig. Filleted strips for trolling or cut up chunks for still fishing will also bring good catches. Keep bait fish in a live bait box that has circulating water.

7. Clams (including mussels and quohaugs) run a close second to worms as the top all-around bait for small salt water fish. Only the meat is used for bait and should be hooked through the tough shell muscle or neck. Still fishing on the bottom usually produces the best results. Carry your clams in a ventilated container lined with wet seaweed. Use those with broken shells first.

FAVORITE GAME FISH

Fortunately, in North America, the problem is not where to find game fish but rather, what species to fish for. Often a single body of water will hold over one hundred different species. With this great abundance, it is only natural that certain fish have become favorites, either for their great fighting ability or a combination of fight, size and eating quality.

Below are listed some of the more popular fresh and salt water game fish, telling how and where to catch them and what baits or lures to use.

Note: Most states require a fishing license and have set seasons on their game fish. Learn what the laws and requirements are before you start fishing.

Fresh Water

Sunfish—These scrappy little fighters supply most young anglers with their first fishing thrills. Small in size, rarely over one and one-quarter pounds, but big in fight and numbers, the sunfish is an excellent choice for light tackle. Many similar species are listed as sunfish making them our most numerous game fish.

Where and How—Geographically, sunfish are found from coast to coast and from southern Canada to the Gulf of Mexico. They favor warm water ponds and lakes, living in and around weedy shallows with overhanging shade from bushes, docks or trees. A small mouth makes small bait or lures necessary.

Baits—Grubs, Nymphs, small pieces of worms, dough balls, corn niblets. Recommended hook sizes are #8-10-12.

Lures—Small flies (wet and dry), small spinners and spoons.

Blue Gill (Bream)—A first cousin to the sunfish only larger, the blue gill is a favorite among fly rod anglers. They have an enormous appetite and will eat just about anything not large enough to eat them. This appetite and their fierce fighting ability make them a good choice for new fishermen.

Where and How—Geographically, the blue gill is found in the same areas and waters as the sunfish. The larger fish tend to locate in deeper water, but rarely over fifteen feet deep. Best fishing is late spring and early summer while they are spawning or guarding the nests. They usually bite best during early morning, late afternoon and evening.

Baits and Lures—Use the same baits and lures recommended for sunfish. On large blue gills, live small minnows (one to one and one-half inches long), grasshoppers, crickets, small plugs and streamers are also used with great success. Recommended hook sizes are #6-8-10.

Crappies (Calico Bass)—As the largest member of the sunfish family, the crappie is a favorite among light tackle and still fishermen. Great numbers and a huge appetite make them easy to catch. In fact, once a school is located it is not uncommon to have a good eating "string" within an hour.

Where and How—Geographically, the crappie enjoys the same range as other members of the sunfish family. Black crappies are usually found in northern waters and weigh one pound or less. White crappies, common to southern waters often weigh two pounds or more. The world's record is over five pounds. Fish for both species in quiet shallow waters (three to eight feet deep) in and around weed beds, stumps, overhanging banks and docks. In rivers, back eddies are a favorite hangout. During the hot summer months, they usually retreat to cooler water fifteen to twenty feet deep. Fishing starts early, around February or March, in southern waters lasting until June or July. In northern waters, April, May and June are the best months. Good fishing, however, can be had any time a school is located, even in winter through the ice.

Baits and Lures—The same bait and lures that catch blue gills work equally well on crappies. Just use larger sizes for bigger fish. Recommended hook sizes are #4-6-8.

Yellow Perch—Great numbers which make them easy to catch and a wonderful flavor are the main reasons yellow perch are so popular among sport and commercial fishermen. Each year fishing trawlers on the Great Lakes net over five million pounds of yellow perch. Another estimated three million pounds are caught by sport fishermen who consider them gourmets' delight.

Where and How—Geographically, yellow perch are native to the eastern and mid-west section of America from southern Canada to the Carolinas. They have, however, been introduced as a new species in many western states. Look for them around sand bars and drop-offs that are close by weeded areas. Also in pools below dams, under bridges, piers, and docks. Fishing is good anytime you locate a school, but is best in spring and fall when they are in shallow water. During the hot summer months, the larger fish move to deeper water. Still fishing, trolling, drifting, and casting produce the best results. Average sizes runs under one pound. Larger fish caught in deeper waters often reach two pounds.

Baits—Small minnows (under two inches), garden worms, grubs, grasshoppers, small crayfish (under two inches), and crickets. Recommended hook sizes are #6-8.

Lures—Wet flies, small streamers in red and white or red and yellow patterns, small spinners, spinner-worm combinations, tiny spoons and plugs.

Largemouth Bass—One of fishing's great thrills is watching a largemouth bass explode up through the surface after a plug. Even when hooked there is a good chance the plug will be flung back at the angler. This type of action plus size have made the largemouth one of our top fresh water game fish.

Where and How—Originally confined to the southeastern states, the largemouth has been introduced to favorable waters all over the world. They prefer warm water lakes and ponds that have shallow bays and coves. Shaded weed beds, lily pads, submerged logs, stumps, and old docks are favorite hangouts. In fact, there is a good chance you will find largemouths anywhere you find sunfish or perch, both a favorite natural food. The northern largemouth rarely goes over five pounds while the southern specie averages eight to ten pounds, lunkers reaching up into the high teens.

Early morning and dusk (late evening) produce the best results when fishing the shallows. Surface plugs and poppers worked slowly with erratic jerks are favorite lures at this time. Fishing during the bright daylight hours can be frustrating because the fish move into deep water and must be teased into striking. A favorite lure at this time is a red and white deep running wounded minnow. Keep retrieving or trolling just above a known deep weeded area, until a bass hits out of sheer "cussidness."

Baits—Large minnows (three to six inches), shiners, frogs, nightcrawlers (worms), crayfish, mice and small eels are only a few of the baits used to catch largemouths. Recommended hook sizes are #2/0 to 6/0.

Lures—Surface, shallow and deep running plugs of all types, spoons, spinners, spinner-worm combinations, jigs, large streamers, bass bugs and flies, plastic worms, eels, and frogs.

Smallmouth Bass—Another great battler, the smallmouth bass, is rated an even better fighter than his big brother the largemouth. When caught with fly rod or other light tackle, the smallmouth must be considered one of our great fresh water game fish.

Where and How—Unfortunately, smallmouth bass need cool waters to survive. This eliminates them from many areas in the south. Their natural habitat is from eastern Canada, south to Alabama and Georgia. Successful stocking programs have, however, brought them to every west and mid-west state that has favorable conditions. Average weight of the smallmouth is about two pounds. They do grow much larger, however, the world's record being over eleven pounds. Look for smallmouths in cool deep rocky lakes and clean, fast rivers and streams. In late spring and early fall, they are found around rocky shallows in lakes and rocky stretches in rivers near deep holes. Early morning and evening are the best fishing hours. Surface and shallow running lures are the best baits. During the hot summer months, fish deep along drop-offs and over rocky weed beds in lakes. In rivers, fish the deep holes and tails of rapids and riffles. Live bait and deep running lures produce the best results in the hot summer months.

Baits and Lures—Use the same baits and lures recommended for largemouth bass plus any large trout lures. Recommended hook sizes are #1 to 4/0.

Pickerel—In classifying the pickerel, he is best described as a temperamental bully. One day he will charge a bait or lure from fifty feet away smashing it with a vengeance, then dart into a weed bed fouling your line. Another day he will follow every lure offered right up to the boat, then turn and swim away. This unpredictable nature and bad temper make him a worthy foe.

Where and How—Geographically, the pickerel is native to eastern United States from Maine to Florida. Few western states have introduced the pickerel because he has the bad habit of overeating fry (young fish) of other game fish. Look for pickerel in the same surroundings that smallmouth bass and sunfish are found (shallow weed beds, lily pads, stumps, old docks). In rivers, they prefer the quiet back eddies. Still fishing with small live fish bait is a favorite way to catch pickerel. For real thrills, however, use light tackle and surface lures.

Baits—Small minnows (two-and-a-half inches or under), small shiners, frogs, crayfish, mice. Because pickerel are basically carnivorous, they seldom are caught on worms or food baits.

Lures—Surface and shallow running plugs, spoons and spinners. A strip of prepared pork rind on the hook of a spoon or spinner often produces when other lures fail.

Northern Pike—A mean disposition, great size, and an unsatiable appetite combine to make the northern pike a much sought after game fish. An average weight of five to seven pounds in waters near population centers jumps to over twenty pounds in remote wilderness areas. The world's record being forty-six pounds two ounces. Unlike the pickerel, who instinctively strike at a bait, northerns stalk their prey like a land tiger by hiding from sight in bottom grasses or weed beds. Only when a victim is lured into a sense of false security do they strike.

When hooked the northern becomes a tenacious battler usually heading for the bottom making you earn back every inch of line. Or on occasions they let you retrieve them like an old shoe, only to explode into action as you go to land them. This trick often leads to a freed fish, a broken rod tip and a mighty "shook-up" fisherman.

Where and How—Geographically, northern pike are found all across the northern United States, Canada and Alaska. They prefer large lakes with good stands of weed beds and lily pads. Early morning and late evening, when they are out hunting, is the best time to fish. During the heat of the day fish cooler waters over deep weed beds. Casting, trolling, and still fishing all produce good results. Heavy tackle with wire leaders is a must unless you are a skilled fly rod or light tackle angler.

Baits—Large minnows, shiners and other bait fish (up to ten inches in length), frogs, mice, or small snakes.

Lures—Large; surface, shallow running and deep running plugs, spoons and spinners. Prepared pork strips or a red bucktail on the hook of a spoon or spinner often produce when other lures fail.

Brook Trout (Square Tail)—Trout and salmon are considered the aristocrats of fresh water game fish. And for thousands of fly fishermen, the brook trout is the prince regent. A great fighter and gourmets' delight, the square tail offers light tackle fishermen, especially fly rod anglers, superb sport fishing.

Where and How—Geographically, the brook trout is native to Northeastern United States and Canada. Heavy stocking programs have, however, introduced him to all suitable waters in the Western states and Western Canada. To survive, the brook trout must have clean, cold waters. Any prolonged water temperature over seventy degrees is usually fatal. Fish for them in fast moving streams and cool spring fed lakes. In streams, look for them in and around riffles and rapids, in the swirls behind large rocks. When resting they lie in deep pools, along the quiet edge of riffles, and under overhanging banks or fallen trees. In lakes look for them near the bottom around cold water springs. Small brookies (under one pound) feed mostly on insects, nymphs and occasional earth worms. Larger brookies (one to five pounds) continue to eat insects and nymphs but also include minnows, and other fish in their diet. Fly fishing with wet and dry flies and streamers are the accepted way to fish for brook trout. Other books will tell you that spinning tackle, even casting tackle with live bait or "hardware" lures produce the biggest fish. This may be true occasionally, but for pure thrills and excitement, use your fly rod and enter the ranks of true sportsmen.

Lures—Trout flies and streamers. Recommended hook sizes #4 to 16.

Other favorite fresh water game fish are listed below. Check with a fisherman friend or local fishing supply dealer to find out if any are in your local waters and how to fish for them.

Atlantic Salmon	Walleye
Landlocked Salmon	White Perch
Brown Trout	Rock Bass
Rainbow Trout	White Bass
Steelhead Trout (sea run)	Catfish
Lake Trout (touge)	Bullheads (Horn Pout)
Muskellunge (Muskie)	Eels
Shad	

Salt Water

Since the end of World War II, salt water fishing has become a major sport, mainly because of better fishing and boating equipment.

Following is a list of some of the more sought after salt water game fish. Check with a fisherman

SUNFISH

YELLOW PERCH

CHAIN PICKEREL

BLUEGILL

LARGEMOUTH BASS

NORTHERN PIKE

CRAPPIE

SMALLMOUTH BASS

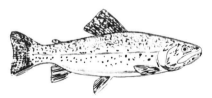

BROOK TROUT

friend or tackle dealer to find out if any are in your coastal waters and how to fish for them.

Striped Bass	Chinnook	Bluefish
Sea Bass	Salmon	Bonefish
Porgy	Pollock	Bonito
Weakfish	Amberjack	Barracuda
Mackerel	Tuna	Grouper
Flounder	Drum	Pompano
Fluke	Tarpon	Snook
Marlin	Sailfish	Red Snapper
	Shark	

WHERE TO LOCATE FISH

Game fish are always found close by food sources and/or hiding places. Normally, in the spring and fall, they are located in shallow waters, while in the heat of summer, as the shallows become warm, they move to cooler and deeper water. The trick is to find these feeding and hiding spots.

Favorite areas to look for game fish are:

Lakes and Ponds

Shallow and deep weed beds, lily pads, stumps, and logs, the mouth and head of streams, around channels and openings in weed beds, along reefs, sand bars and ledges that drop off to deeper water, and under overhanging banks, bushes or trees.

Rivers and Streams

The first rule of stream fishing is, stay hidden as much as possible. Shadows or a fisherman's body are sure ways to scare off fish that live in narrow, shallow waterways.

In slow waters, fish the deep pools, around sunken logs and fallen trees, along undercuts in banks, back eddies, and tails of riffles, also under overhanging bushes and trees.

In fast waters, fish the quiet waters found behind large rocks, fallen trees or log jams. Fish like to rest in these areas because they don't have to fight the current but still can dash out to grab food as it swims or drifts by. Also fish the pools below rapids, in and around eddies where currents sweep by bends and rocky areas.

When fishing streams and rivers, cast upstream and let the lure or bait float by naturally through the area you want to cover. Then when retrieving the lure, which will be downstream, try to imitate the action of bait fish.

Salt Water

Docks, piers and bridges are excellent salt water fishing spots. The marine growth attached to the underwater pilings of these structures creates a good food source for bait fish which in turn attract game fish. Still fishing with live or food bait produces the best results.

When trolling or surf casting, look for feeding

sea birds or moving swirls or chop. This is often a sign large fish have driven bait fish to the surface. Work these areas with live bait or artificial lures that resemble the bait fish in the water.

Tides are also an important factor as many game fish move in and out over tidal flats after small fish and other food as the water rises and falls. Check with local fishermen and bait dealers for the best time to fish the tides.

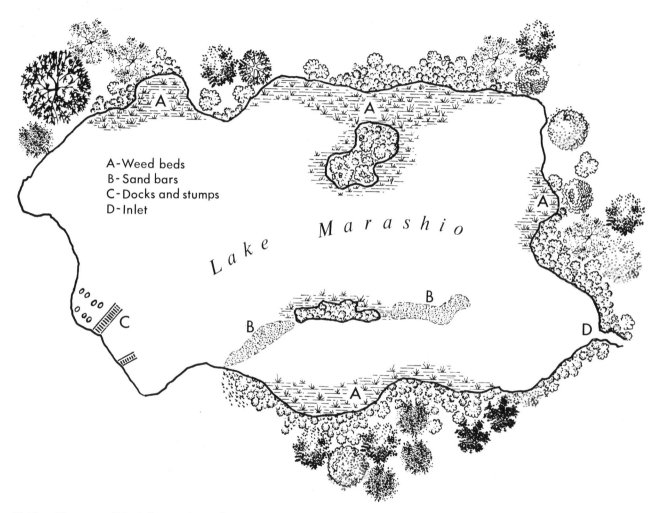

A-Weed beds
B-Sand bars
C-Docks and stumps
D-Inlet

Lake Marashio

Fishing "hot spots" in lakes and ponds.

64